CHRISTMAS SONGS
FOR CLASSICAL PIANO

15 SEASONAL GEMS ARRANGED BY PHILLIP KEVEREN

— PIANO LEVEL —
LATE INTERMEDIATE

ISBN 978-1-4950-9437-8

7777 W. BLUEMOUND RD. P.O. BOX 13819 MILWAUKEE, WI 53213

Visit Hal Leonard Online at
www.halleonard.com

Visit Phillip at
www.phillipkeveren.com

PREFACE

Every Christmas delivers a new holiday song or two – some from recording artists, others from films or Broadway musicals. Only a precious few of these offerings turn out to be evergreen. The songs in this collection have proven to be perennial favorites, and will likely continue to float on the crisp Yuletide air for many seasons to come.

Using classical compositional devices, these favorite songs have been developed into character pieces for piano solo.

Merry Christmas,

Phillip Keveren

BIOGRAPHY

Phillip Keveren, a multi-talented keyboard artist and composer, has composed original works in a variety of genres from piano solo to symphonic orchestra. Mr. Keveren gives frequent concerts and workshops for teachers and their students in the United States, Canada, Europe, and Asia. Mr. Keveren holds a B.M. in composition from California State University Northridge and a M.M. in composition from the University of Southern California.

CONTENTS

ALL I WANT FOR CHRISTMAS IS YOU

(with J.S. Bach's Invention No. 10, BWV 781)

Words and Music by MARIAH CAREY
and WALTER AFANASIEFF
Arranged by Phillip Keveren

Briskly (♩. = 104)

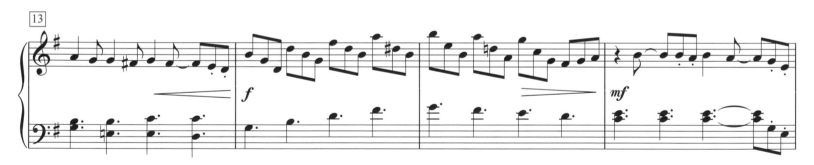

THE CHRISTMAS SONG
(Chestnuts Roasting on an Open Fire)

Music and Lyric by MEL TORME and
ROBERT WELLS
Arranged by Phillip Keveren

Deeply expressive, with rubato ($\bullet$ = c. 56)

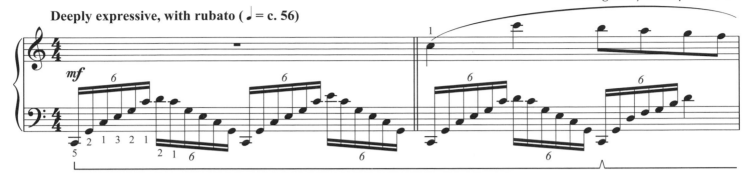
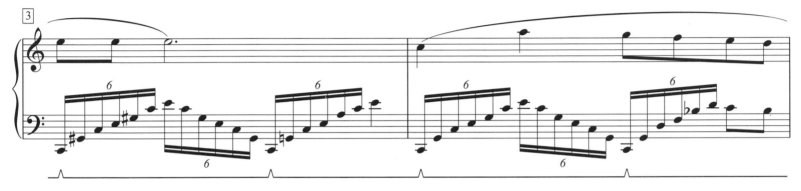
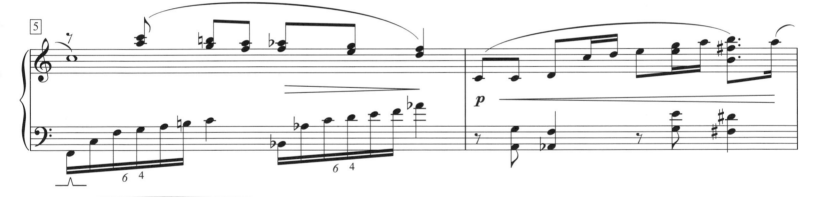
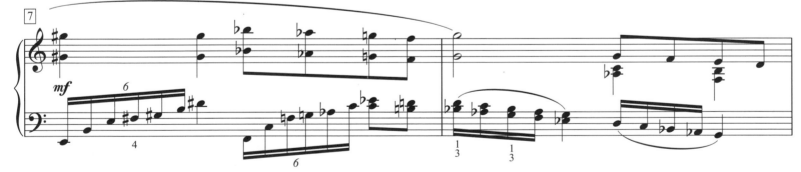

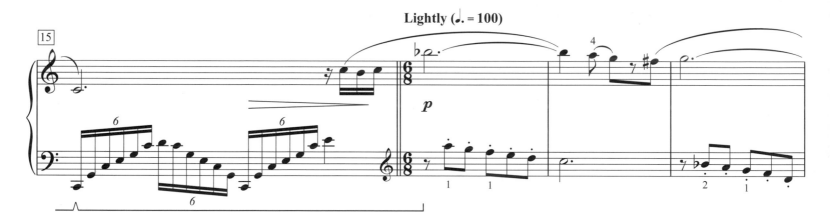

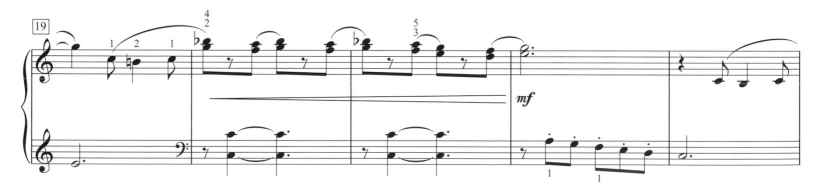

Tempo I (♩ = c. 56)

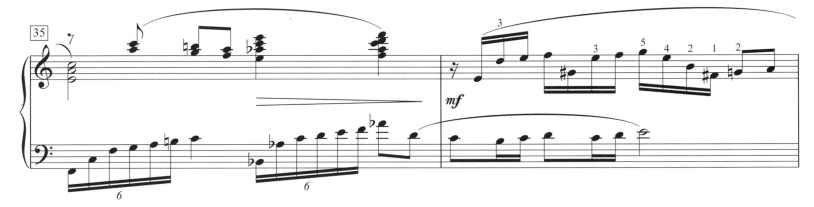

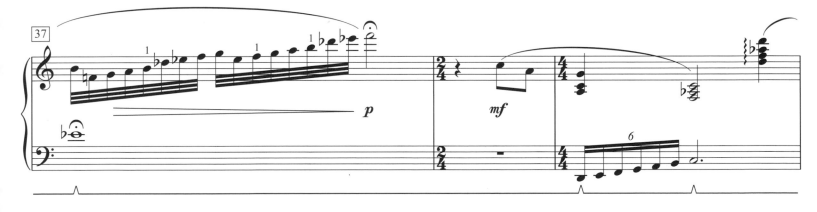

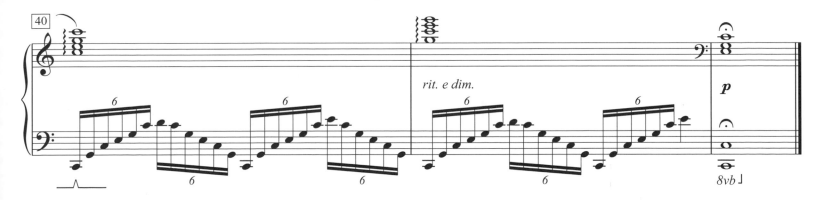

THE CHRISTMAS WALTZ

Words by SAMMY CAHN
Music by JULE STYN
Arranged by Phillip Keveren

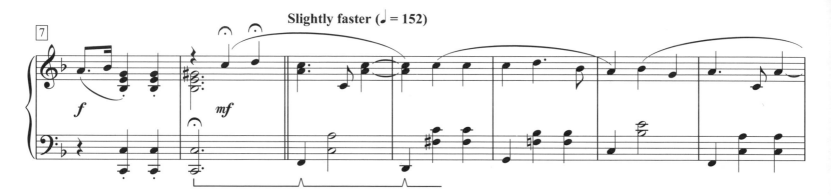

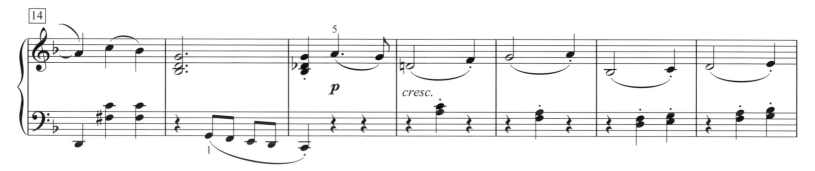

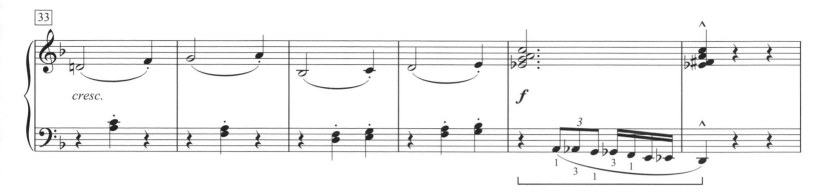

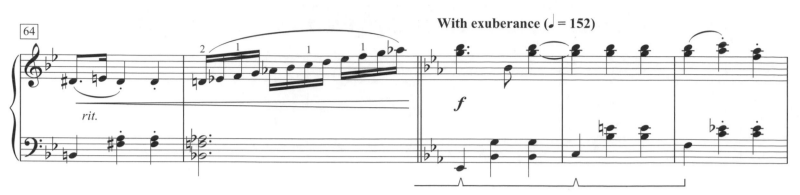

With exuberance (♩ = 152)

HERE COMES SANTA CLAUS
(Right Down Santa Claus Lane)

Words and Music by GENE AUTRY
and OAKLEY HALDEMAN
Arranged by Phillip Keveren

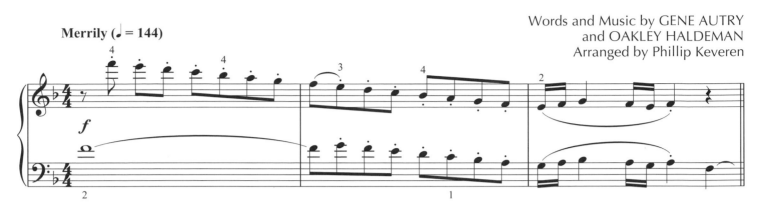

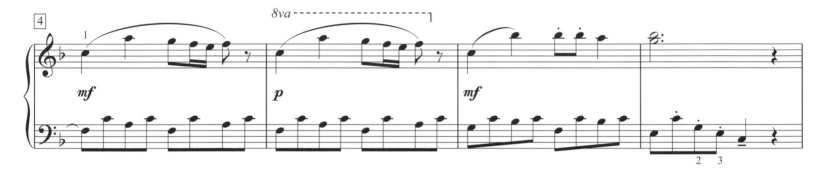

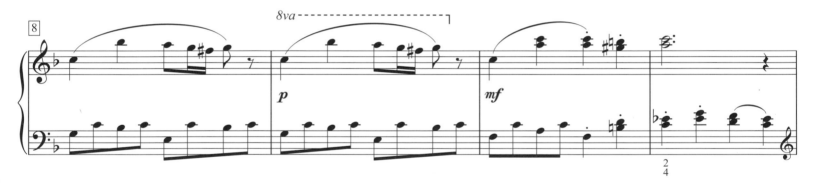

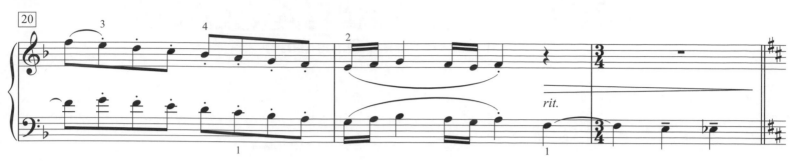

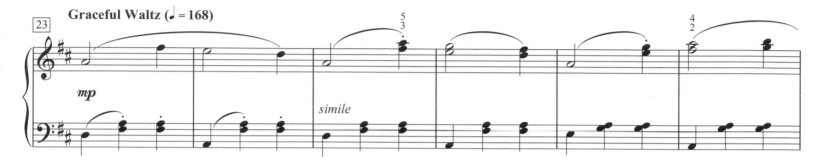

Graceful Waltz (♩ = 168)

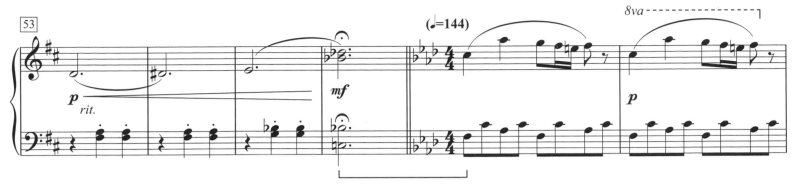

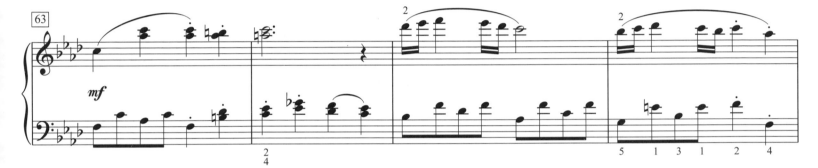

HAVE YOURSELF A MERRY LITTLE CHRISTMAS

from MEET ME IN ST. LOUIS

Words and Music by HUGH MARTIN
and RALPH BLANE
Arranged by Phillip Keveren

Allegro (♩ = 120-126)

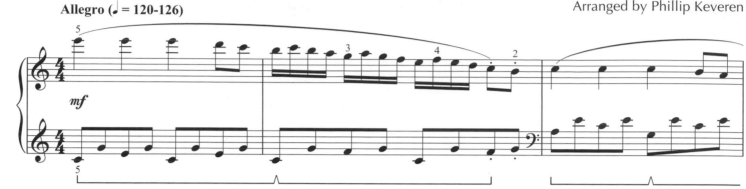

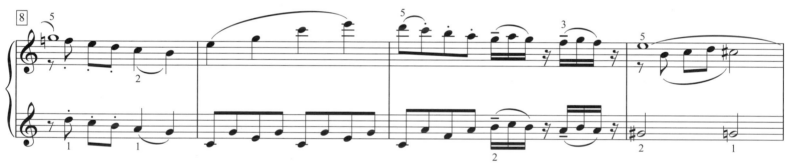

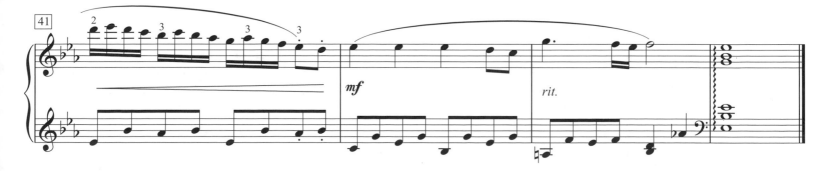

I'LL BE HOME FOR CHRISTMAS

(inspired by Chopin's Prelude in E minor, Op. 28, No. 4)

Words and Music by KIM GANNON
and WALTER KENT
Arranged by Phillip Keveren

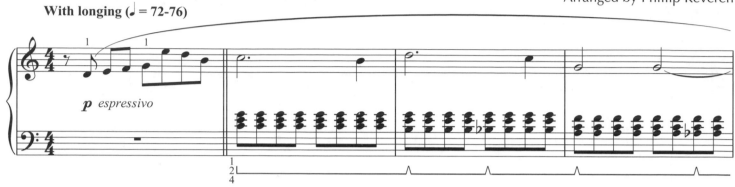

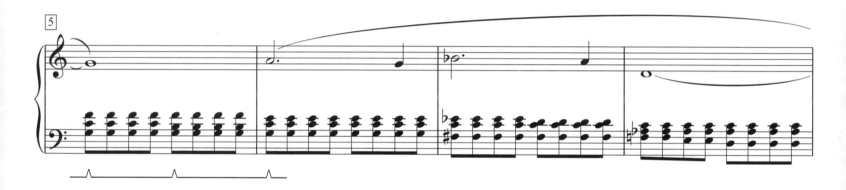

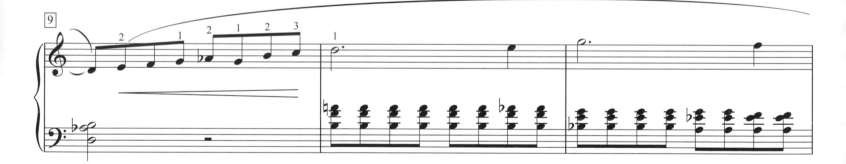

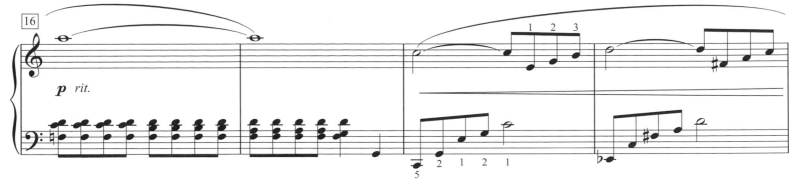

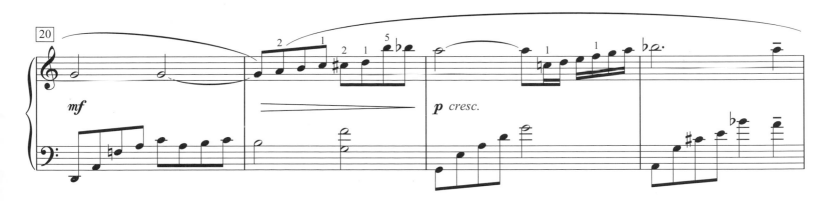

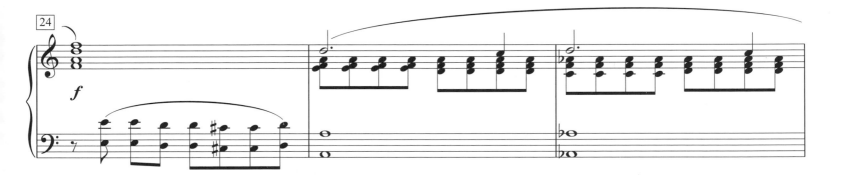

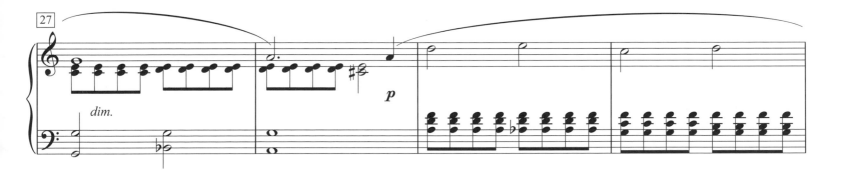

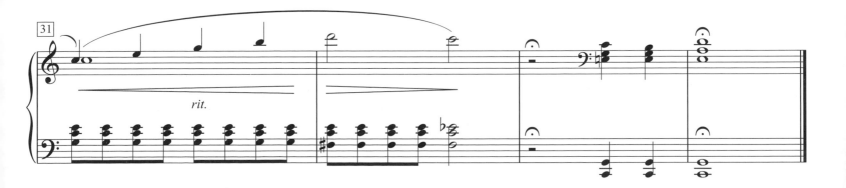

JINGLE BELL ROCK
(with Scarlatti's Sonata in C major, K. 460)

Words and Music by JOE BEAL
and JIM BOOTHE
Arranged by Phillip Keveren

MERRY CHRISTMAS, DARLING

Words and Music by RICHARD CARPENTER
and FRANK POOLER
Arranged by Phillip Keveren

Rubato (♩ = c. 80)

pedal liberally

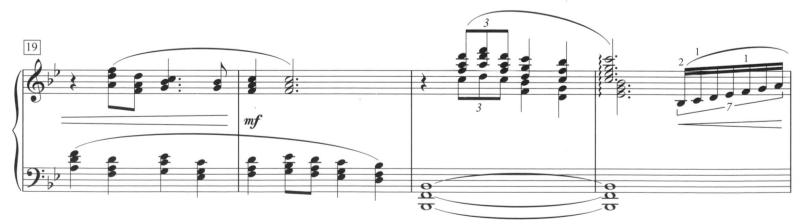

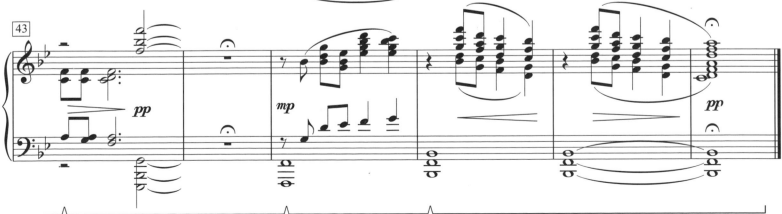

THE MOST WONDERFUL TIME OF THE YEAR

(with Tchaikovsky's "Waltz of the Flowers" from *The Nutcracker*)

Words and Music by EDDIE POLA
and GEORGE WYLE
Arranged by Phillip Keveren

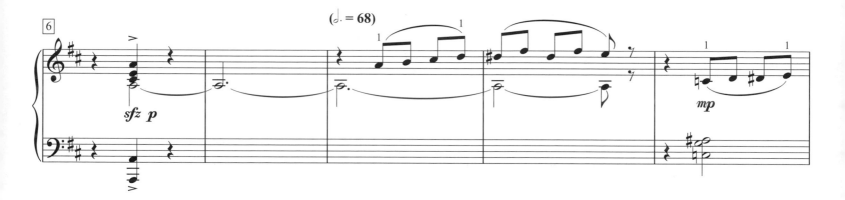

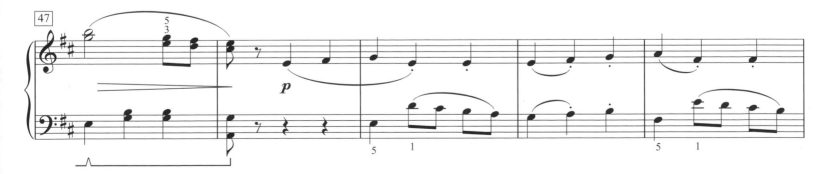

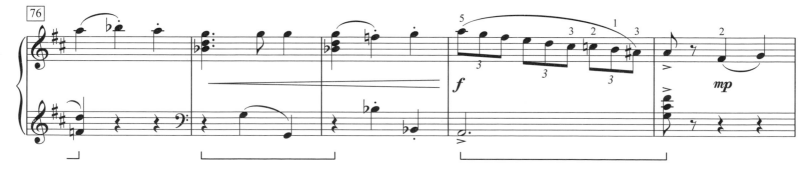

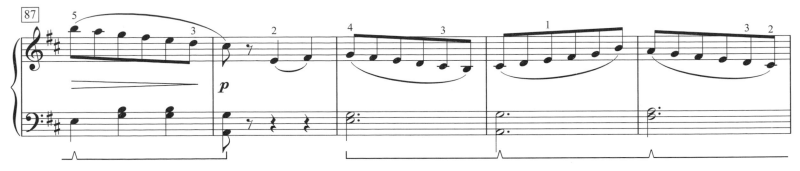

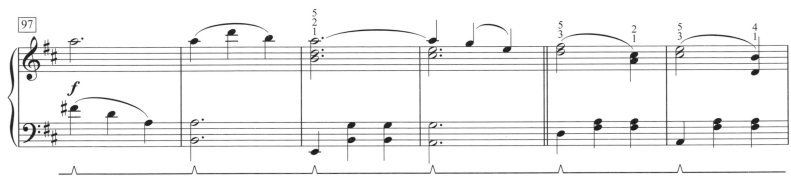

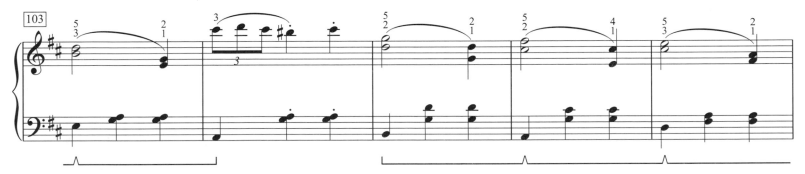

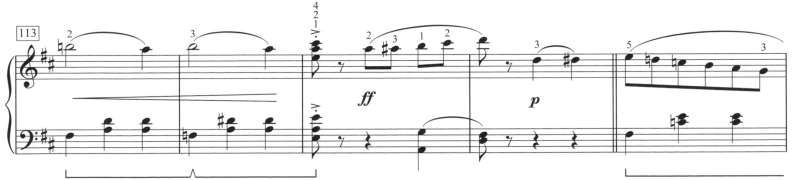

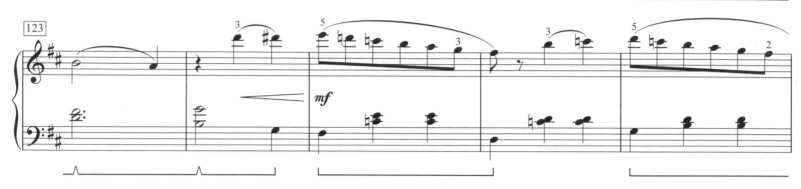

SANTA CLAUS IS COMIN' TO TOWN

Words by HAVEN GILLESPIE
Music by J. FRED COOTS
Arranged by Phillip Keveren

Jolly Jig (Gigue) (♩. = 108)

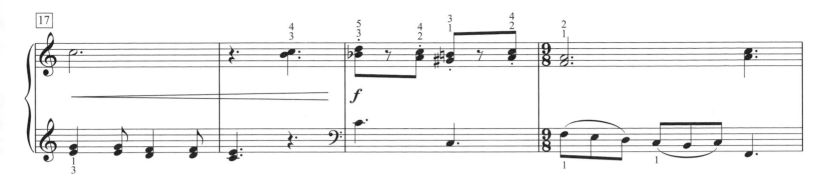

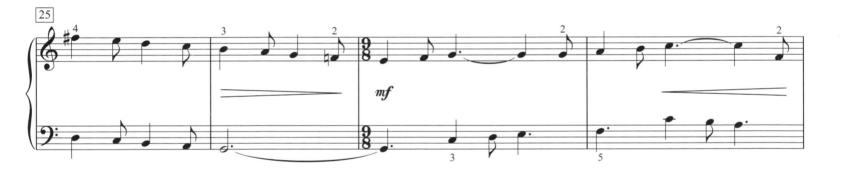

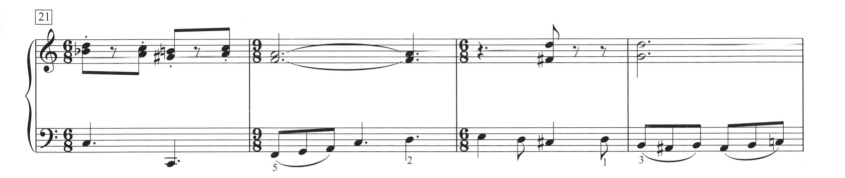

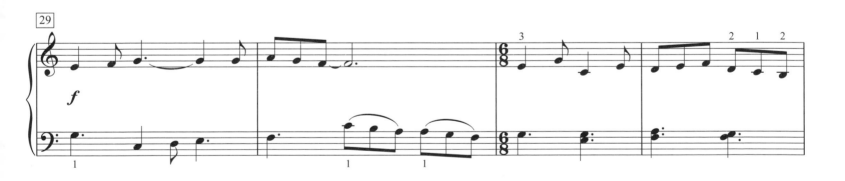

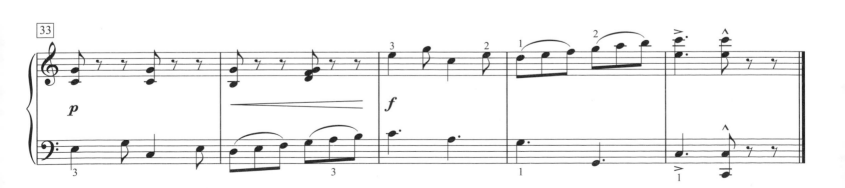

SILVER BELLS
from the Paramount Picture THE LEMON DROP KID

Words and Music by JAY LIVINGSTON
and RAY EVANS
Arranged by Phillip Keveren

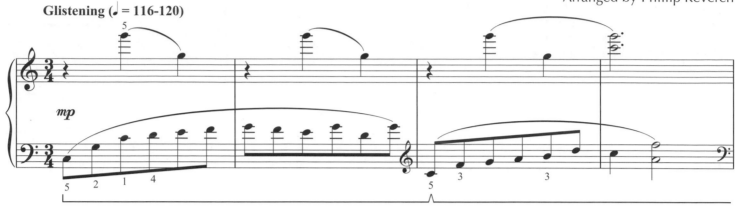

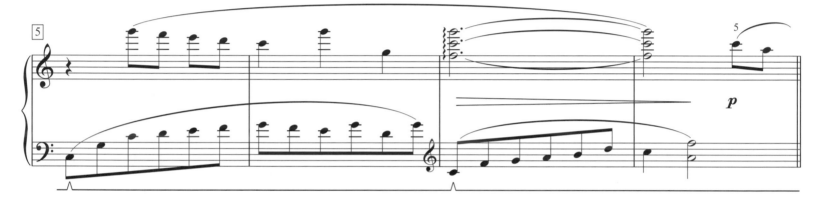

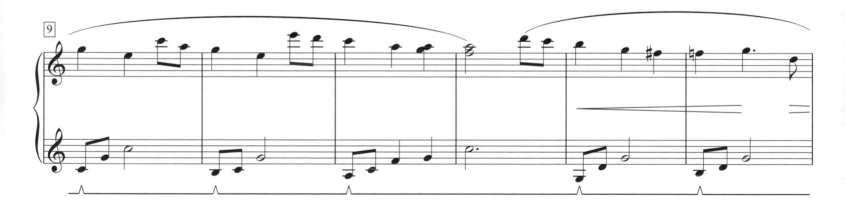

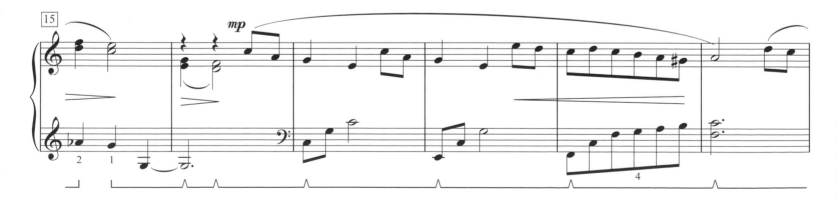

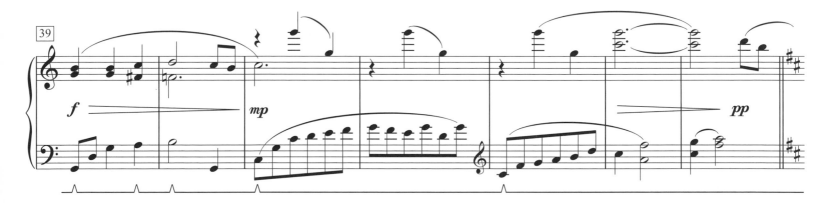

SNOWFALL
(inspired by Debussy's "En bateau" from *Petite Suite*)

Lyrics by RUTH THORNHILL
Music by CLAUDE THORNHILL
Arranged by Phillip Keveren

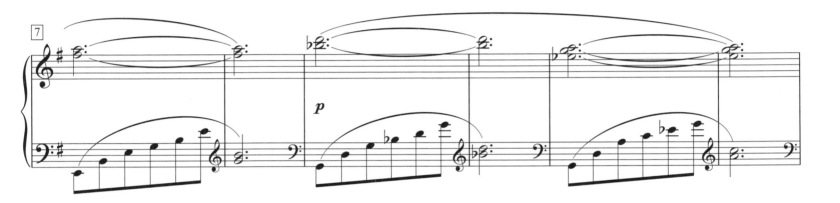

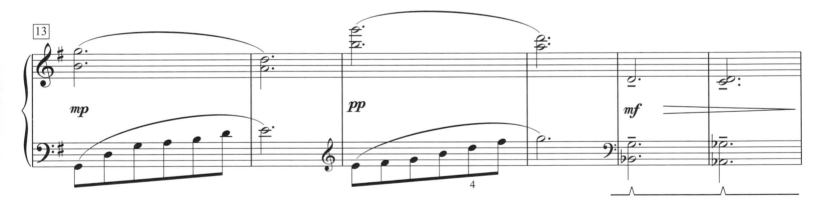

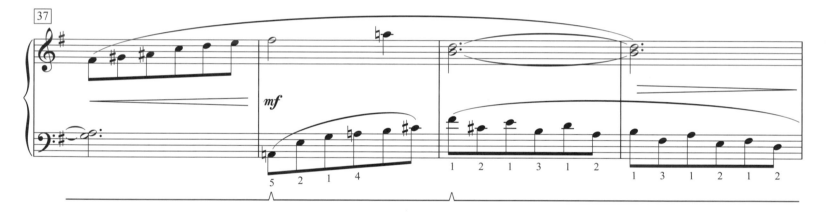

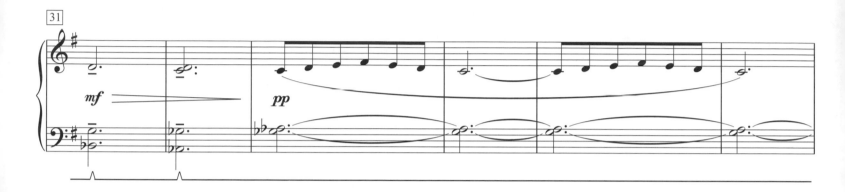

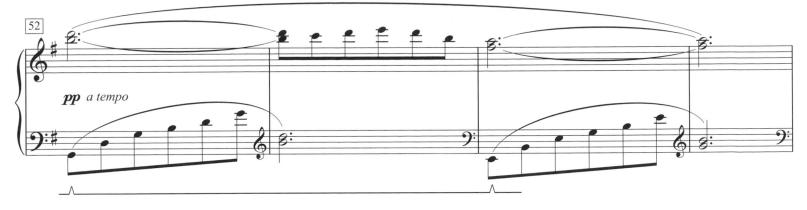

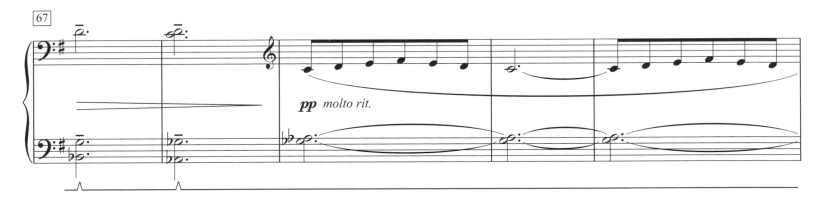

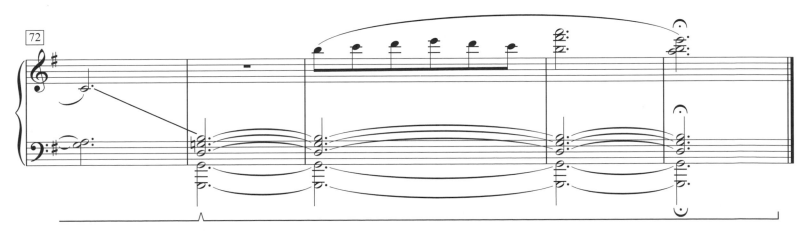

SOMEWHERE IN MY MEMORY
from the Twentieth Century Fox Motion Picture HOME ALONE

Words by LESLIE BRICUSSE
Music by JOHN WILLIAMS
Arranged by Phillip Keveren

WHERE ARE YOU CHRISTMAS?

from DR. SEUSS' HOW THE GRINCH STOLE CHRISTMAS
(with Clementi's Sonatina in C Major, Op. 36, No. 3)

Words and Music by WILL JENNINGS,
JAMES HORNER and MARIAH CAREY
Arranged by Phillip Keveren

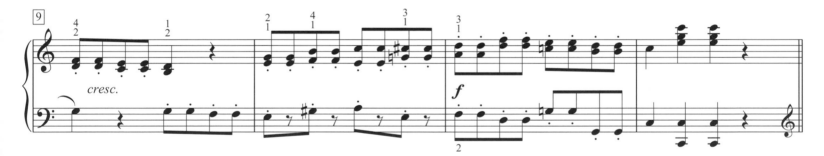

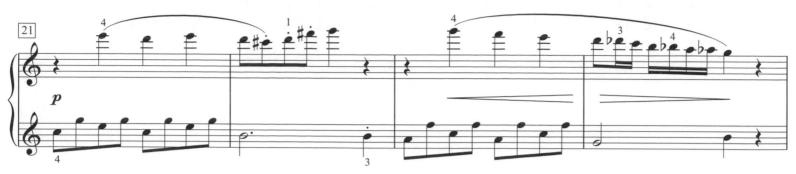

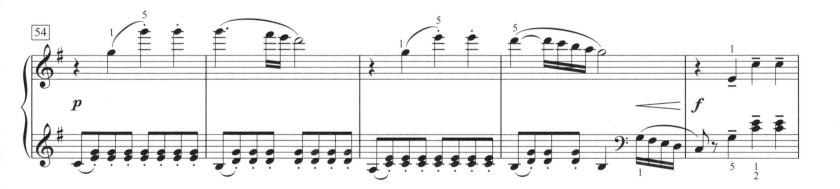

WHITE CHRISTMAS
from the Motion Picture Irving Berlin's HOLIDAY INN

Words and Music by IRVING BERLIN
Arranged by Phillip Keveren

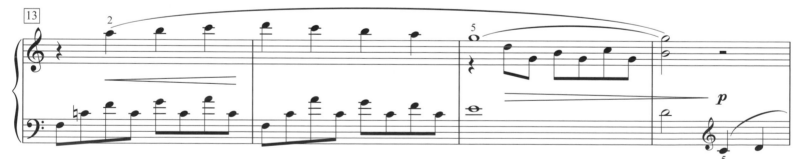

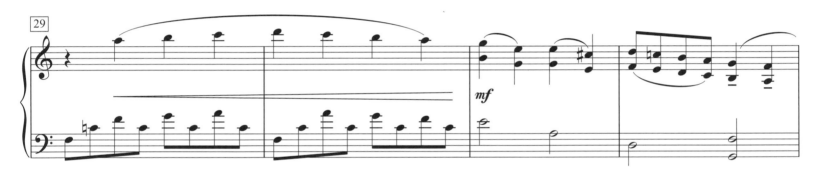

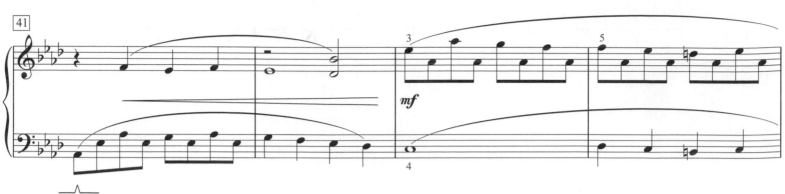

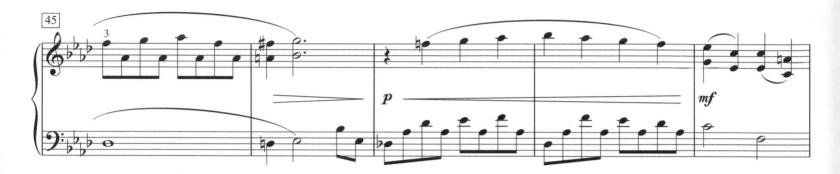

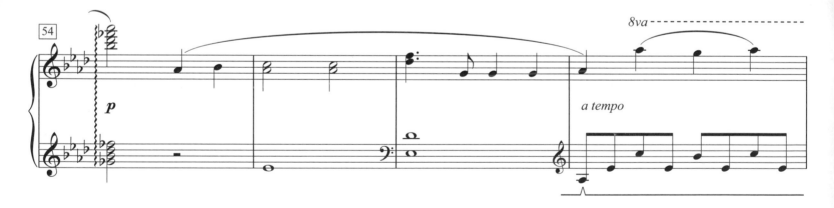

THE PHILLIP KEVEREN SERIES

CHRISTMAS COLLECTIONS
FROM HAL LEONARD
ALL BOOKS ARRANGED FOR PIANO, VOICE & GUITAR

THE BEST CHRISTMAS SONGS EVER

69 all-time favorites: Auld Lang Syne • Coventry Carol • Frosty the Snow Man • Happy Holiday • It Came Upon the Midnight Clear • O Holy Night • Rudolph the Red-Nosed Reindeer • Silver Bells • What Child Is This? • and many more.
00359130 ....$29.99

THE BIG BOOK OF CHRISTMAS SONGS

Over 120 all-time favorites and hard-to-find classics: As Each Happy Christmas • The Boar's Head Carol • Carol of the Bells • Deck the Halls • The Friendly Beasts • God Rest Ye Merry Gentlemen • Joy to the World • Masters in This Hall • O Holy Night • Story of the Shepherd • and more.
00311520 ....$22.99

CHRISTMAS SONGS – BUDGET BOOKS

100 holiday favorites: All I Want for Christmas Is You • Christmas Time Is Here • Feliz Navidad • Grandma Got Run Over by a Reindeer • I'll Be Home for Christmas • Last Christmas • O Holy Night • Please Come Home for Christmas • Rockin' Around the Christmas Tree • We Need a Little Christmas • What Child Is This? • and more.
00310887 ....$14.99

CHRISTMAS MOVIE SONGS

34 holiday hits from the big screen: All I Want for Christmas Is You • Believe • Christmas Vacation • Do You Want to Build a Snowman? • Frosty the Snow Man • Have Yourself a Merry Little Christmas • It's Beginning to Look like Christmas • Mele Kalikimaka • Rudolph the Red-Nosed Reindeer • Silver Bells • White Christmas • You're a Mean One, Mr. Grinch • and more.
00146961 ....$19.99

CHRISTMAS PIANO SONGS FOR DUMMIES®

56 favorites: Auld Lang Syne • Away in a Manger • Blue Christmas • The Christmas Song • Deck the Hall • I'll Be Home for Christmas • Jingle Bells • Joy to the World • My Favorite Things • Silent Night • more!
00311387 ....$19.95

CHRISTMAS POP STANDARDS

22 contemporary holiday hits, including: All I Want for Christmas Is You • Christmas Time Is Here • Little Saint Nick • Mary, Did You Know? • Merry Christmas, Darling • Santa Baby • Underneath the Tree • Where Are You Christmas? • and more.
00348998 ....$14.99

CHRISTMAS SING-ALONG

40 seasonal favorites: Away in a Manger • Christmas Time Is Here • Feliz Navidad • Happy Holiday • Jingle Bells • Mary, Did You Know? • O Come, All Ye Faithful • Rudolph the Red-Nosed Reindeer • Silent Night • White Christmas • and more. Includes online sing-along backing tracks.
00278176 Book/Online Audio $24.99

CHRISTMAS SONGS FOR KIDS

28 favorite songs of the season, including: Away in a Manger • Do You Want to Build a Snowman? • Here Comes Santa Claus (Right down Santa Claus Lane) • Mele Kalikimaka • Rudolph the Red-Nosed Reindeer • Santa Claus Is Comin' to Town • Silent Night • Somewhere in My Memory • and many more.
00311571 ....$12.99

100 CHRISTMAS CAROLS

Includes: Away in a Manger • Bring a Torch, Jeannette, Isabella • Coventry Carol • Deck the Hall • The First Noel • Go, Tell It on the Mountain • I Heard the Bells on Christmas Day • Joy to the World • O Come, All Ye Faithful (Adeste Fideles) • Silent Night • Sing We Now of Christmas • and more.
00310897 ....$19.99

100 MOST BEAUTIFUL CHRISTMAS SONGS

Includes: Angels We Have Heard on High • Baby, It's Cold Outside • Christmas Time Is Here • Do You Hear What I Hear • Grown-Up Christmas List • Happy Xmas (War Is Over) • I'll Be Home for Christmas • The Little Drummer Boy • Mary, Did You Know? • O Holy Night • White Christmas • Winter Wonderland • and more.
00237285 ....$24.99

POPULAR CHRISTMAS SHEET MUSIC: 1980-2017

40 recent seasonal favorites: All I Want for Christmas Is You • Because It's Christmas (For All the Children) • Breath of Heaven (Mary's Song) • Christmas Lights • The Christmas Shoes • The Gift • Grown-Up Christmas List • Last Christmas • Santa Tell Me • Snowman • Where Are You Christmas? • Wrapped in Red • and more.
00278089 ....$17.99

A SENTIMENTAL CHRISTMAS BOOK

27 beloved Christmas favorites, including: The Christmas Shoes • The Christmas Song (Chestnuts Roasting on an Open Fire) • Christmas Time Is Here • Grown-Up Christmas List • Have Yourself a Merry Little Christmas • I'll Be Home for Christmas • Somewhere in My Memory • Where Are You Christmas? • and more.
00236830 ....$14.99

ULTIMATE CHRISTMAS

100 seasonal favorites: Auld Lang Syne • Bring a Torch, Jeannette, Isabella • Carol of the Bells • The Chipmunk Song • Christmas Time Is Here • The First Noel • Frosty the Snow Man • Gesù Bambino • Happy Holiday • Happy Xmas (War Is Over) • Jingle-Bell Rock • Pretty Paper • Silver Bells • Suzy Snowflake • and more.
00361399 ....$24.99

A VERY MERRY CHRISTMAS

39 familiar favorites: Blue Christmas • Feliz Navidad • Happy Xmas (War Is Over) • I'll Be Home for Christmas • Jingle-Bell Rock • Please Come Home for Christmas • Rockin' Around the Christmas Tree • Santa, Bring My Baby Back (To Me) • Sleigh Ride • White Christmas • and more.
00310536 ....$14.99

Complete contents listings available online at www.halleonard.com

PRICES, CONTENTS, AND AVAILABILITY SUBJECT TO CHANGE WITHOUT NOTICE.

0621
302